心之道

The force of a vow
Benefitting oneself and others
by generating bodhicitta

發菩提心，自利利他

第三輯

心道法師 語錄

y Dharma
laster Hsin Tao

目錄

Contents

作者簡介

心道法師一九四八年生，祖籍雲南，幼失依怙，為滇緬邊境孤雛。十三歲隨孤軍撤移來台，十五歲初聞觀音菩薩聖號，有感於觀音菩薩的悲願，以「悟性報觀音」、「吾不成佛誓不休」、「真如度眾生」刺身供佛，立誓

The force of a vow
Benefitting oneself and others
by generating bodhicitta

願力篇
智慧法語

徹悟真理，救度苦難。

　二十五歲出家後，頭陀行腳歷十餘年，前後在台北外雙溪、宜蘭礁溪圓明寺、莿仔崙墳塔、龍潭公墓和員山周舉人廢墟，體驗世間最幽隱不堪的「塚間修」，矢志修證，了脫生死，覺悟本來。

生道場」，展開弘法度
生的佛行事業，為現代
人擘劃成佛地圖。為了
推動宗教共存共榮，法
師以慈悲的華嚴理念奔
走國際，並於二〇〇一
年十一月成立世界宗教
博物館，致力於各種不
同宗教的對話，提昇對
所有宗教的寬容、尊重

和感恩，期能達到地球一家、世界和平。

在佛化教育推動上，心道法師以「四期教育」作為培育僧才、教導信眾的教化體系，從個人到群體，有次第、有方向地教育僧信如何精進。「四期教育」包括「阿含期」

著重基礎佛法戒、定、
慧的學習與薰陶，建立
佛法生活規範；「般若
期」著重在明瞭與貫徹
空性智慧；「法華期」
著重生起願力，發菩提
心；「華嚴期」則強調
多元共存、和諧共生，
證入圓滿無礙的境界。

　　心道法師以禪的

Brief Introduction to the Author

Born in upper Myanmar in 1948 to ethnic Chinese parents of Yunnan Province, Master Hsin Tao was left orphaned and impoverished at an early age. Having

The force of a vow
Benefitting oneself and others
by generating bodhicitta

願力篇
智慧法語

been taken in by
the remnants of
ROC military units
operating along the
border of Yunnan,
China, he was brought
to Taiwan in 1961
when he was 13. At
the age of 15, he was

deeply moved by
the compassion of
Guanyin Bodhisattva
(Avalokiteśvara)
and resolved to seek
the supreme truth
and to bring relief
to all who suffer.
As an offering to

the Buddha, he had
himself tattooed
with the vows
"May I awaken
in gratitude for
the kindness of
Guanyin," "I will
never rest until
Buddhahood is

enlightenment, Master Hsin Tao traveled on foot for over ten years, practicing austerities in lonely and secluded locations, including Waishuangxi in Taipei, Yuanming

meaning of "Only
when all beings
are liberated, is
enlightenment fully
attained." Standing
on the summit of the
Ling Jiou Mountain,
looking down at
the Pacific Ocean,

Master Hsin Tao felt
great compassion
for the suffering of
all sentient beings.
After his solitary
retreat he established
the Wusheng Monastery
on the mountain in
order to propagate

strived hard to
gain international
support with the
compassionate spirit
of the Buddhist
Avatamsaka Vision (of
the interconnectedness
of all beings in
the universe), and

is dedicated to
advancing the cause
of world peace
and a promoting
awareness of our
global family for
love and peace
through interreligious
dialogues. The

practice. First comes the āgama stage, which centers on the foundational teachings of Buddhism and the three-fold practice of morality, concentration, and wisdom. The prajñā

stage emphasizes the
theory and practice
of emptiness. The
dharmapuṇḍarīka
stage focuses on the
bodhisattva practice
of developing the
mind of enlightenment
through the power

The force of a vow
Benefitting oneself and others
by generating bodhicitta

願力篇
智慧法語

Master Hsin Tao has devoted himself to propagating the Dharma through education, based on the Chan principle of quieting the mind and seeing one's original Buddha-

The force of a vow
Benefitting oneself and others
by generating bodhicitta

commitment, he
leads people to
devote themselves
to the great cause
of benefiting all
sentient beings,
ceaselessly helping
them achieve liberating
truth through

心之道第三輯 智慧法語

願力篇－發菩提心，自利利他

The Way of Mind III:
Words of wisdom

The force of a vow :
Benefitting oneself and others
by generating bodhicitta

願力就是財富。

The force of a vow
Benefitting oneself and others
by generating bodhicitta

The force of a vow is a kind of wealth.

The force of a vow
Benefitting oneself and others
by generating bodhicitta

願力篇
智慧法語

Bodhicitta is the aspiration
to cultivate unbounded
wisdom for the sake of
all sentient beings.

The force of a vow
Benefitting oneself and others
by generating bodhicitta

願力篇
智慧法語

With the force of a vow,
you diligently forge onwards,
unrestrained by views about
time and space.

因眾生而生起大悲心；
因大悲心而生起菩提心；
因菩提心而成就正覺。

The force of a vow
Benefitting oneself and others
by generating bodhicitta

智慧法語 願力篇

The existence of
sentient beings gives rise
to great compassion;
great compassion gives rise
to bodhicitta;
bodhicitta gives rise
to enlightenment.

The force of a vow
Benefitting oneself and others
by generating bodhicitta

Respecting
all sentient beings
amounts to paying homage
to all the Buddhas.

每個人都是你的一畝田，
想要豐收，
必須努力種植、耕耘。

The force of a vow
Benefitting oneself and others
by generating bodhicitta

願力篇
智慧法語

Other people are
your field of merit;
by diligently cultivating it
you are sure to enjoy
a bountiful harvest.

The force of a vow
Benefitting oneself and others
by generating bodhicitta

Practicing compassion
brings happiness to both
oneself and others.

學佛的人，
第一要悟明心性，
第二則是發起無量慈悲心。

The first step
in Buddhist practice is
recognizing the nature of
the mind; the second step
is cultivating the mind of
unlimited compassion.

The force of a vow
Benefitting oneself and others
by generating bodhicitta

願力篇
智慧法語

The ten great vows of
Samantabhadra are
the most effective way of
putting the Bodhisattva path
into practice.

The force of a vow
Benefitting oneself and others
by generating bodhicitta

Treading the Bodhisattva
path is our vow;
recollection of the Buddha
is our practice.

以「寂靜」
爲心智開發；
以「慈悲」
讓成佛的心不退轉。

The force of a vow
Benefitting oneself and others
by generating bodhicitta

Set out with tranquility as
your source of wisdom;
stay on the path with
compassion as your guide.

The force of a vow
Benefitting oneself and others
by generating bodhicitta

By merely avoiding evil and
practicing goodness,
you are bound to cultivate
many wholesome affinities.

The force of a vow
Benefitting oneself and others
by generating bodhicitta

願力篇
智慧法語

Every day be sure to
benefit yourself and others
by accumulating merit and
generating bodhicitta.

Treading the Bodhisattva
path means serving others.

佛法就像是
生活的潤滑劑，
如果你不使用佛法，
生活就會轉不動。

The force of a vow
Benefitting oneself and others
by generating bodhicitta

The Buddha-dharma is
the lubricant of life;
without it,
things get stuck.

要常常把心布施出來，
當一個神聖且
自利利他的使者。

The force of a vow
Benefitting oneself and others
by generating bodhicitta

願力篇
智慧法語

Constantly practice
generosity;
make yourself an
ambassador of giving.

隨緣，
就是不管身處何處，
都能適應環境，
更能正念不移。

The force of a vow
Benefitting oneself and others
by generating bodhicitta

願力篇
智慧法語

According with circumstances means mindfully adapting to whatever situation you happen to be in without wavering on the path.

將佛法傳給眾人，
一起學習佛法的
無上智慧。

The force of a vow
Benefitting oneself and others
by generating bodhicitta

願力篇
智慧法語

Propagate the Dharma
by cultivating
the supreme wisdom of
the Buddha-dharma
together with others.

能夠散播佛法的種子，
這才是眞正的幸福。

The force of a vow
Benefitting oneself and others
by generating bodhicitta

願力篇
智慧法語

Propagating
the Buddha-dharma is
genuine happiness.

要有善的循環，

彼此才可以互相造福；

如果互相傷害，

生生世世就是交煎受苦。

The force of a vow
Benefitting oneself and others
by generating bodhicitta

Never miss an opportunity
to cultivate goodness and
harmonious relations with
others; engaging in conflict
with others only brings
misery, life after life.

The force of a vow
Benefitting oneself and others
by generating bodhicitta

願力篇
智慧法語

All sentient beings
are our spiritual guides;
everywhere you turn,
you find an opportunity
to cultivate wisdom.

多從人緣、
愛心方面下功夫，
不要找一個敵對的對象，
讓自己障礙。

The force of a vow
Benefitting oneself and others
by generating bodhicitta

Make a concerted effort
to always get along well
with others; don't create
obstacles for yourself
by making enemies.

Setting out with a vow
worthy of a Buddha,
you return to
the realm of Amitābha.

The force of a vow
Benefitting oneself and others
by generating bodhicitta

Only with the intention
to deliver all sentient beings
is it possible to
cultivate unlimited wisdom;
only with unlimited wisdom
is it possible to
attain Buddhahood.

有多大的願力，
就有多大的成就；
有多大的慈悲，
就有多大的果報。

The force of a vow
Benefitting oneself and others
by generating bodhicitta

The greater your vow,
the greater your success;
the greater your compassion,
the greater your results.

The force of a vow
Benefitting oneself and others
by generating bodhicitta

願力篇 智慧法語

Bodhicitta consists of
generosity, morality,
patience, energy,
concentration, and wisdom.

The force of a vow
Benefitting oneself and others
by generating bodhicitta

Where do supportive
conditions come from?
They are the result of
making a vow.

只要有一位眾生不成佛，
有一位父母親友沒有度脫，
就是我們的苦。

The force of a vow
Benefitting oneself and others,
by generating bodhicitta

As long as a single sentient
being remains in saṃsāra,
we ourselves still suffer.

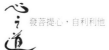

正面、愛心、
積極、願力，
要以此落實於修行，
並以佛法待人。

The force of a vow
Benefitting oneself and others
by generating bodhicitta

Proper practice is based on
a positive attitude,
a loving heart,
energetic striving, and
the force of a vow;
use the Buddha-dharma
to get along with others.

The force of a vow
Benefitting oneself and others
by generating bodhicitta

願力篇
智慧法語

In treading
the Bodhisattva path,
you have to have a sense of
purpose and direction;
each step brings
its own results.

The force of a vow
Benefitting oneself and others
by generating bodhicitta

願力篇
智慧法語

Karma is the present result
of past action;
the cause is in the past,
the result is in the present.

The force of a vow
Benefitting oneself and others
by generating bodhicitta

願力篇
智慧法語

Everybody has
the Buddha-nature;
the attainment of
Buddhahood begins with
making a vow.

The force of a vow
Benefitting oneself and others
by generating bodhicitta

智慧法語 願力篇

By chanting the Great
Compassion Mantra and
cultivating the mind of
loving kindness
you become
a manifestation of Guanyin.

「自覺」就是
讓自己不惑；
「覺他」是
讓別人不惑；
「覺行圓滿」就是
讓這兩個都圓滿。

"Self-awakening" means
making an end of confusion;
"awakening others" means
helping others
to do the same;
"perfection of awakening"
means bringing both of
these to completion.

發菩提心就是遍智，
也是學佛人生生世世
的生命志業。

The force of a vow
Benefitting oneself and others
by generating bodhicitta

願力篇 智慧法語

Generating bodhicitta,
you incline in the direction
of pervasive wisdom;
this is the resolution of
the Buddhist aspirant,
life after life.

The force of a vow
Benefitting oneself and others
by generating bodhicitta

願力篇
智慧法語

Always striving
to benefit others
makes your good fortune
sustainable.

The force of a vow
Benefitting oneself and others
by generating bodhicitta

願力篇
智慧法語

Deal with all conditions
with modesty and humility.

The force of a vow
Benefitting oneself and others
by generating bodhicitta

There's no reaping
without first sowing;
now is the time
to sow wholesome seeds.

要對佛法生起信心，
重點在實踐，
沒有實踐等於空想。

The force of a vow
Benefitting oneself and others
by generating bodhicitta

願力篇
智慧法語

You may have faith
in the Buddha,
but if you don't
follow it up with action,
then it amounts to nothing
but a pipe dream.

生死無常，
要創造永恆的生命，
就要結善緣、學佛。

The force of a vow
Benefitting oneself and others
by generating bodhicitta

Life and death are
impermanent.
Practicing the Dharma and
cultivating wholesome
affinities is the way
to attain eternal life.

The force of a vow
Benefitting oneself and others
by generating bodhicitta

The mind of the Bodhisattva
is characterized by
loving kindness, compassion,
sympathetic joy,
and equanimity.

The force of a vow
Benefitting oneself and others
by generating bodhicitta

願力篇
智慧法語

By taking
the Buddha-dharma
as your guide,
you can work without
generating defilements,
and without getting
embroiled in conflict.

Repent for whatever
misdeeds you may have
committed in body, speech,
or mind; realize the
essentially empty nature of
both good and evil;
generate the heart of great
compassion.

Recite the mantra
"Amitābha" and
do good deeds;
this is the best way
to avoid catastrophe.

願力就是
跟苦難在一起，
推動慈悲的法，
依願力去做。

With the force of a vow,
you have the presence of
mind to remain compassionate,
even when facing
serious difficulties.

我們沒辦法掌控無常，
只能依照佛法學習，
獲得智慧與解脫。

The force of a vow
Benefitting oneself and others
by generating bodhicitta

願力篇
智慧法語

Impermanence is beyond our control; what we can do is practice according to the Buddha's teaching, and cultivate the wisdom which brings liberation.

The force of a vow
Benefitting oneself and others
by generating bodhicitta

Properly practicing
recollection of the Buddha
has nothing to do with
mindless muttering;
rather, it means bringing
the Buddha's unconditional
love into every aspect of
life.

The force of a vow
Benefitting oneself and others
by generating bodhicitta

願力篇
智慧法語

Taking joy
in the virtues of others
encourages them
to cultivate a good heart;
take every opportunity
to inspire others
to practice the Dharma.

The force of a vow
Benefitting oneself and others
by generating bodhicitta

願力篇
智慧法語

With universal compassion
as your guiding principle,
you have unbounded
energy and life becomes
meaningful.

The force of a vow
Benefitting oneself and others
by generating bodhicitta

By dedicating the merit
arising from
your good deeds to
the wellness of
all sentient beings,
you lay down positive
affinities and the basis for
happiness.

心之道第三輯智慧法語
願力篇-發菩提心，自利利他

心道法師語錄
總 策 劃：釋了意
主　　編：洪淑妍
責任編輯：林玉芬
英文翻譯：甘修慧
英文審校：Dr. Maria Reis Habito
美術設計：蒲思元
發 行 人：歐陽慕親
出版發行：財團法人靈鷲山般若文教基金會附設出版社
劃撥帳戶：財團法人靈鷲山般若文教基金會附設出版社
劃撥帳號：18887793
地址：23444新北市永和區保生路2號21樓
電話：(02)2232-1008
傳真：(02)2232-1010
網址：www.093books.com.tw
讀者信箱：books@ljm.org.tw
法律顧問：永然聯合法律事務所
印刷：大亞彩色印刷製版股份有限公司
初版一刷：2014年7月
定價：新台幣250元(1套4冊)
ISBN：978-986-6324-76-5
總 經 銷：飛鴻國際行銷有限公司

靈鷲山書網

The Way of Mind Ⅲ : Words of wisdom

The force of a vow : Benefitting oneself and others by generating bodhicitta

Words of Dharma Master Hsin Tao

General Planer: Ven.Liao Yi Shih

Editor in Chief: Hong, Shu-yan

Editor in Charge: Lin, Yu-fen

English translator: Gan, Xiu-hui

English Proofooding: Dr. Maria Reis Habito

Art Editor: Pu, Szu-Yuan

Publisher: Ouyang, Mu-qin

Published by and The postal service is allocated: the Subsidiary Publishing House of the Ling Jiou Mountain Prajna Cultural Education Foundation

Account number: 18887793

Address: 21F., No.2, Baosheng Rd., Yonghe Dist., New Taipei City 23444, Taiwan (R.O.C.)

Tel: (02)2232-1008

Fax: (02)2232-1010

Website: www.093books.com.tw

E-mail: books@ljm.org.tw

Legal Consultant: Y. R. Lee & Partners Attorneys at Law

Printing: Apex Printing Corporation

The First Printing of the First Edition: July 2014

List Price: NT$ 250 dollars(Four-Manual Set)

ISBN: 978-986-6324-76-5

Distributor : Flying Horn International Marketing Co., Ltd.

國家圖書館出版品預行編目(CIP)資料

心之道智慧法語. 第三輯 / 洪淑妍主編.--初版.
-- 新北市 : 靈鷲山般若出版, 2014. 07
　　冊 ;　　公分
ISBN 978-986-6324-76-5(全套 : 精裝)

1. 佛教說法 2. 佛教教化法

225. 4　　　　　　　　　　　　　103011796